A GUIDE FOR ADULT CHILDREN OF ALCOHOLIC PARENTS

LEWIS DANIELSON

Table of Contents

Introduction

The effects of having alcoholic parents on a child are significant and long-lasting. Because alcoholism is such a pervasive problem, affecting numerous families around the world, the frequency with which people go through this is sometimes understated. Children living in such homes face a wide range of difficulties that have long-lasting effects on their development.

The emotional toll on children is one of the most obvious effects. They are subjected to a chaotic home life full of fighting and uncertainty since their parents are alcoholics. Children of alcoholics or those prone to violence or emotional breakdowns may be exposed to these behaviors at home. A person's emotional health can be permanently damaged by traumatic situations that induce feelings of fear, worry, and powerlessness.

Growing up with alcoholic parents can have far-reaching consequences. Disruptions to these kids' regular routines and lack of basic care are a common problem. Due to parents' preoccupation with their drinking, children of alcoholics often go unattended and receive inconsistent care. Because of this, they may not get the proper nourishment, practice good hygiene, or attend school on a consistent basis, all of which might stunt their growth.

Children of alcoholics are more likely to struggle with substance misuse problems themselves, both now and in the future. Children who are raised in households where alcohol is abused may internalize this standard and turn to substance use as a coping mechanism or as an adult.

And the effects of growing up with alcoholic parents can last even into adulthood. Problems with trust, low self-esteem, and the inability to build meaningful relationships are common among the adult children of alcoholics. Some of the ways that people show the effects of childhood trauma are through anxiety disorders, sadness, and suicidal tendencies.

Despite these difficulties, it's vital to remember that not everyone who grows up with alcoholic parents ends up with serious repercussions. Some people are able to overcome their traumatic experiences with the help of counselling, support groups, or caring relationships. Alcoholism is a destructive cycle, but it may be broken with the right help and a solid support system.

It will take a multipronged strategy to reduce the prevalence and consequences of having drunk parents. It entails getting the word out, spreading preventative education, and making sure people in need have access to mental health services. Society can help those who grew up in a home with an alcoholic parent break the cycle and have a better future by providing them with support and tools.

Having parents who drank heavily can have far-reaching consequences for a child's health and happiness later in life. Poor school performance may result from a combination of factors, including a chaotic home life, parents who aren't actively involved, and sporadic encouragement to study. These difficulties might make it harder for a youngster to focus, maintain motivation, and reach his or her academic potential.

Growing up with alcoholic parents has repercussions for the whole family, not just the child who endured it. Relationships between siblings might become strained as they work through the challenges posed by their parents' alcoholism. They may try to play parents, feel sibling rivalry or jealousy, and have difficulty developing close relationships with their siblings. The instability and emotional well-being of the children is further disrupted when the alcoholic parents' marriage is put under stress, which can lead to increasing conflict, separation, or divorce.

Another common result of drunkenness in the household is monetary instability. To buy alcohol or pay for medical care for alcohol-related health problems can drain resources that could be used to provide for a family's basic requirements. Because of this, children may have an even harder time getting by, which might result in things like less chances to participate in extracurricular activities and fewer visits to the doctor.

The social repercussions of being raised by alcoholics need to be recognized as well. Growing up in such conditions can be challenging for kids, and they may have trouble finding their place in the world. It may be difficult for them to develop meaningful connections, keep a steady job, and positively impact their communities. A dysfunctional cycle may be perpetuated, affecting not just the current generation but also the next.

The value of early detection and preventative measures cannot be overstated. The potential harm to children can be lessened by assisting at-risk families as soon as possible. Parenting classes, lessons on stress management, and dealing with emotional issues can all play a role in helping people stop drinking.

Individuals, families, communities, and society at large must all work together to end alcoholism's destructive cycle within families. We can establish a society that fosters resilience, promotes recovery, and guarantees a brighter future for individuals who have grown up with alcoholic parents by prioritizing the well-being of children, offering comprehensive support services, and working towards prevention.

The road to recovery from the damage done by alcoholic families is a long and winding one. It calls for bravery, introspection, and the guts to face the hurt from one's past. Individuals can free themselves from their pasts, reimagine who they are, and forge new connections through acts of forgiveness, self-care, and exploration. By taking this path to recovery, people not only help themselves, but also pave the way for a more accepting and empathetic world for those who have also struggled with addiction. The rest of this book will be focused on all you need to know about breaking the effects that your parent's alcoholism has had on you.

Chapter one

The generational effects of alcoholism

Addiction is a multidimensional disease that can be passed down through families and continue to have severe effects. Addiction is a cycle that involves many causes, both internal and external, making it difficult to break free of its grip.

The person battling addiction is key to this vicious cycle. Addiction typically develops as an attempt to alleviate psychological distress. The transient relief afforded by addictive substances or activities, such as gambling or other compulsive behaviors, provides a compelling escape. However, the effects wear off quickly, creating a loop of needing more and more of the substance to achieve the same effect.

Addiction's effects can be felt through the generations in a family. Addiction affects the family structure, making it more likely that children will observe dysfunctional coping techniques, be neglected, or be subjected to physical, emotional, or sexual abuse. These traumatic events can affect a person's mental and emotional health for the rest of their lives.

Addiction can also be passed on from generation to generation due to genetic factors. The risk of acquiring addictive behaviours may be higher in people with certain genetic predispositions. The brain's reward system, sensitivity to drugs, and emotional regulation abilities are just a few of the traits that can be affected by one's genes. Consequently, offspring of addicts are more likely to share their parents' genetic susceptibility for developing addiction.

The environment also plays a role in the transmission of addiction from one generation to the next. An individual's vulnerability to drug use, stress, and access to treatment is heavily influenced by their family and social networks as well as their socioeconomic status. One's opinion of substance use and their propensity to experiment with it might be shaped by their upbringing, and the presence or acceptance of addiction in their community.

Children who grew up with parents who struggled with addiction may unwittingly carry on those parents' destructive behaviours into adulthood. As individuals seek relief from their emotional burdens through the use of addictive substances or behaviours, the cycle continues. This environment is then passed on to their own children, who are at a higher risk of developing addiction as a result.

An integrated strategy is necessary to break the addictive loop. The first step is to educate the public about addiction and its repercussions. Addiction treatment should centre on alleviating the psychological suffering that often precedes substance abuse. We can help people break the vicious cycle by encouraging healthy coping strategies and teaching them alternate methods to deal with stress and emotions.

Family therapy and other forms of social support, such as peer support groups, may also prove important. These groups can help reduce the feelings of isolation that are commonly associated with addiction by providing a secure environment in which members can open up to one another about their struggles and get practical and emotional assistance.

Equally crucial is working to alter the larger social climate in which addiction flourishes. Implementing policies that prioritise prevention and early intervention, as well as decreasing the stigma associated with substance abuse, are all necessary steps in this direction.

Addiction is a complex disease with generational effects, and by understanding this, we can begin to break the cycle. The next generation can be healthier and more resilient if we help individuals and families overcome addiction through compassion, empathy, and robust support structures.

It is essential to address the underlying issues that contribute to the transmission of addiction across generations if we are to succeed in breaking the cycle of addiction once and for all. This calls for a comprehensive strategy that addresses the addict as a whole, as well as their immediate and extended networks.

Promoting open communication and understanding within the family unit is a first step towards healing and rehabilitation. In the safe space of therapy, family members can communicate openly and trust can be restored. Both the person with the addiction and their loved ones can learn to recognise dysfunctional habits and replace them with better coping mechanisms.

Addiction is a destructive cycle, but education can help break it. People can make better decisions about their own health and the health of their loved ones by learning more about the risks associated with substance abuse and addictive behaviours. Substance addiction prevention programmes that are both effective and comprehensive should be a joint effort of educational institutions, community groups, and medical professionals.

Those at risk can avoid the progression of addictive behaviours if they receive intervention and support early on. Counselling, therapy, and drug and alcohol rehabilitation programmes can help with this. An individual's ability to overcome addiction and heal from traumatic experiences and subsequent ineffective coping mechanisms can be greatly enhanced by early intervention.

Addiction is a cycle that can only be broken with the help of the community. A sense of community and belonging can be cultivated through the development of strong support networks and the provision of safe places where people can openly discuss their challenges and triumphs. Ongoing encouragement, assistance, and accountability are provided by peer support groups, community centres, and recovery organisations.

To break the addiction cycle that can be passed down through families, societal adjustments are required. Reducing the availability and accessibility of addictive substances and expanding access to effective treatment options should be important goals of policy. More resources should be allocated to studying addiction, more people should have access to healthcare, and harm reduction measures should be put into place.

It is critical to take on addiction head-on by addressing the underlying social and economic causes. In order to reduce the prevalence of substance abuse, it is necessary to address issues such as unemployment, poverty, and social injustice. We can make our communities less hospitable to the emergence and maintenance of addiction if we invest more in areas like social support, education, and economic possibilities for all members of society.

Addiction is a cycle that can only be broken through a concerted effort on the part of individuals, families, communities, and the larger society. An atmosphere where people who are battling with addiction are met with compassion, empathy, and the resources they need to rehabilitate requires a change in mindsets, policies, and support systems. Individuals can be given the tools they need to live happier, healthier lives and create a better world for future generations if we can break the cycle of intergenerational trauma.

Recovery is a lifelong process, and we must keep that in mind as we work to end the cycle of addiction. Maintaining sober and avoiding relapse calls for continuous assistance and resources. Long-term sobriety necessitates participation in an aftercare programme, residing in a sober living community, and maintaining contact with a counsellor or support group.

Efforts to prevent problems also need to be prioritised. We can lessen the risk of addiction forming in the first place by emphasising early intervention, encouraging healthy coping mechanisms, and building community resilience. Addiction can be prevented with the use of awareness programmes that dispel harmful beliefs about substance use, provide useful communication and problem-solving skills, and instill a healthy sense of self-worth in the target audience.

Reversing the effects of addiction requires treating any underlying mental health issues that may be present. Addiction is often accompanied by other mental health concerns, such as depression, anxiety, or a traumatic disorder. Long-term sobriety and ending the cycle of addiction in one's family require multifaceted treatment plans that address both substance abuse and mental health issues simultaneously. Mental health care, psychiatric treatment, and trauma-informed therapies are all part of this.

The social stigma of addiction must be overcome if any real progress is to be made. Addiction is a vicious cycle that is kept going because people are too ashamed to ask for help. It is possible to lessen the shame people feel when they seek help for substance abuse by promoting an atmosphere of compassion, openness, and acceptance.

Special difficulties that adult offspring of alcoholics often go through

The effects of having alcoholic parents on a child might linger long after the child becomes an adult. The special difficulties that adult offspring of alcoholics confront can have a lasting impact on their emotional, psychological, and relationship health.

The battle to trust one another is one of the greatest obstacles. It might be challenging for adult children to trust others if they grew up in a home where their parents' behaviour was erratic and often influenced by alcohol. They may have learned to be sceptical of others' intentions and dread being let down as a result of their own experiences with betrayal, emotional manipulation, and inconsistent parental support.

Managing your guilt and shame is another obstacle you may face. It is common for adult offspring of alcoholics to internalise blame for their parents' addiction and come to believe that they are to blame for their parents' actions. They could feel bad about wanting to cut ties with their parents or for being helpless in the face of the situation. Feelings of guilt and shame can weigh a person down, making it hard to feel confident in oneself and build positive bonds with others.

Adult children of alcoholics have a more complicated time establishing healthy boundaries. Because their parents couldn't provide for them, they might have had to raise themselves or their siblings from an early age. They may have trouble as adults prioritising their own needs and creating boundaries because they have learned to put the needs of others before their own. The result may be an inability to stand up for oneself in social and professional settings, or a practise of codependence.

Adult children of alcoholics often struggle with emotional management. The ability to develop good coping mechanisms and emotional regulation abilities can be stunted by living in a chaotic and unpredictable environment. They could have trouble calming themselves, articulating how they feel, or simply knowing what they need. This might show as aversion to confrontation, repression of feelings, or the opposite extreme, severe overreaction.

Adult offspring of alcoholics often find it difficult to form close, trusting connections with others. They may have had trouble building attachments as children because they grew up in homes where interpersonal relationships were tense or absent. It's possible that they have issues with being vulnerable, with abandonment anxiety, or with repeatedly choosing partners who are also addicted.

Adult children of alcoholics may also struggle with issues of self-care and self-worth. They may not have been taught the importance of looking for themselves as children. They may have trouble prioritising their own needs, establishing healthy boundaries, and seeing their own value as a result. Problems with self-care, a propensity to overwork or please others, and a low opinion of oneself are all symptoms that may emerge.

As a result of their upbringing, adult offspring of alcoholics encounter a wide range of difficulties. Some of the most common challenges they have are difficulties with trusting others, feeling guilty or ashamed, creating boundaries, controlling their emotions, developing close connections, taking care of themselves, and valuing themselves. These people absolutely must find help, go to counselling, and work on themselves if they ever hope to overcome their struggles and live happy, productive lives.

Adult children of alcoholics may likewise have trouble finding their own sense of self. They may not have received the kind of emotional support and guidance they would have needed to discover and pursue their own hobbies, passions, and ambitions while growing up in a home where their parents' addiction dominated centre stage. Sometimes people struggle as adults with figuring out who they are, what they believe in, and why they're here.

Adult offspring of alcoholics may also have to deal with financial instability. Whether it's a lost job, unpaid bills, or misplaced priorities, addiction can wreak havoc on a family's finances. Thus, adult children may have been exposed to financial instability throughout their upbringing, which may have far-reaching consequences for their own financial security as adults. Due to the lack of financial stability they witnessed as children, they may have difficulty managing money, sticking to a budget, or deciding on a solid career path. Adult offspring of alcoholics tend to struggle with their own mental health. They may be more likely to encounter anxiety, depression, or substance misuse problems as adults because of the stress, emotional turbulence, and instability they endured as children. They may also be more likely to turn to unhealthy habits like substance abuse or self-harm.

Even in maturity, family dynamics and relationships can remain tense. In an effort to keep the peace or prevent additional strife, adult children may continue to play the role of caretaker or mediator in their families. This continuous duty can be taxing, and it can cause friction in the family. It can be difficult to set healthy boundaries and manage family interactions when emotional wounds from childhood still linger.

It can take a lifetime to overcome the effects of having parents who drank too much. Breaking toxic patterns calls for introspection, treatment, social support, and determination. Adult children, with time and effort, may overcome trauma, build good relationships, and achieve happiness in all aspects of their lives.

It's crucial to remember that although these difficulties are shared by many adult children of alcoholic parents, each person will encounter their own unique set of issues. Society can help those with substance use disorders recover and prosper, therefore ending the generational cycle of addiction, if more people would only take the time to learn about the problem and show some compassion.

Adult children of alcoholics frequently suffer from feelings of loss and bereavement. They may be pining for the safe and loving upbringing they were denied. They may lament the loss of a stable parental figure and the unrealized potential for joyful childhood memories. Grief and loss must be worked through before one may heal and go on.

The effects of having alcoholic parents might extend into the sphere of one's beliefs and values. Children who are now adults may have doubts about God or find it difficult to make sense of their lives. Children of addicts often struggle with feelings of wrath and contempt directed at a higher power. It may be helpful for them to investigate spirituality and locate a belief system that fits with their ideals.

Adult offspring of alcoholics should prioritise developing a strong support system. Meeting people who can relate to one's situation can help one feel less alone and more at ease opening up about one's struggles. The resources and sense of community provided by support groups, counselling, and community organisations can be invaluable as they face their difficulties.

For adult offspring of alcoholics, breaking the cycle of addiction is a constant struggle. Their upbringing may have predisposed them to a higher chance of acquiring substance misuse problems or indulging in addictive behaviours. A dedication to self-awareness, self-care, and, if necessary, professional support, is necessary to break free from this cycle. Taking deliberate action to improve health and learn effective coping strategies may be required.

Adult offspring of alcoholics often show great endurance and strength in the face of the many obstacles they must overcome. By going through adversity, one can learn compassion, sympathy, and insight into the human condition. Many people who have struggled with addiction go on to become advocates for addiction education, recovery advocates, or mental health professionals.

The path to self-discovery, healing, and growth for the adult child of an alcoholic parent is a long and winding one. It's about rediscovering who they are, calming their nerves, and reconnecting with others in positive ways. They will succeed in spite of the difficulties they face if they are given the resources, encouragement, and care they need.

How these families share certain traits and coping strategies

Some people's unique coping styles, emotions, and behaviours are the direct result of having grown up in an alcoholic home. Addiction is a persistent presence in these households, contributing to an environment of instability and unpredictability. To adapt and survive in such a hostile setting, children often share certain traits and coping techniques with one another.

Hypervigilance seems to be a recurring theme. When you have an alcoholic parent or guardian, you may need to keep a close eye on their mental and physical health. Children raised in such homes develop a keen awareness of even the most minute signs of tension or danger. Their heightened awareness serves as a defence mechanism, allowing them to foresee and avoid potentially explosive circumstances.

A sense of responsibility that exceeds one's years is another trait that matures over time. Because their addicted parent is either absent or untrustworthy, children in alcoholic homes often take on adult responsibilities. They could try to bring some order and consistency into the turmoil by taking on caregiving responsibilities like cooking, cleaning, or watching younger siblings. Their sense of identity and their capacity to set appropriate limits may be shaped by their early adoption of adult responsibilities.

Family members of alcoholics adopt a wide range of coping tactics, most of which centre on staying alive. Children in these situations often resort to denial as a coping method. In an effort to keep up appearances and shield the family name, they may try to downplay or deny the extent of the addiction problem. As a defence mechanism against the aching truth they must face every day, denial is adopted.

Escapism is yet another form of coping that can take many forms. Some people may seek refuge from their troubled family lives by immersing themselves in academics, athletics, or extracurricular activities. Others may try to psychologically escape their situations by daydreaming, reading, or indulging in other alone pursuits. Substance abuse and other addictive behaviours may emerge as a last resort for people who have observed abusive relationships.

Having to rely on oneself is a coping strategy that develops out of necessity. Those who grow up in homes where alcoholism is prevalent generally develop a strong sense of independence and resourcefulness. Since turning to an addict for help is risky and often unsuccessful, children of addicts may develop skills in problem resolution, self-soothing, and emotional regulation on their own. This independence can show up as a resistance to assistance or a preference to keep one's guard up. People who grew up in alcoholic homes are resilient and adaptive, and their shared traits and strategies for dealing with adversity are evidence of this. Recognising these interplays helps pave the way for more compassion, understanding, and effective treatments in their recovery and development.

Characteristics and coping methods learned in alcoholic households may persist in these people even as they enter adulthood. Because their expectations and behaviours are shaped by the dynamics they witnessed in the family unit, individuals may have trouble creating and sustaining good relationships.

Those who grew up in alcoholic homes may find it difficult to form close relationships. They may find it hard to open up and form close relationships because they have trust difficulties, are afraid of being vulnerable, and are very sensitive to potential conflict or abandonment. To further impede the growth of close connections, the self-reliance developed as a youngster can contribute to a reluctance to rely on others or seek support.

A person's sense of self-worth and self-esteem may also suffer in an alcoholic family. Addiction-saturated environments can cause children to develop a warped sense of self-worth, shame, and guilt. They may begin to feel unworthy or imperfect because they blame themselves for their parent's alcoholism. If they have low self-esteem, it can be difficult for them to achieve happiness and success in their lives.

Adaptive coping strategies in an alcoholic family may have negative consequences elsewhere. When people leave the unstable conditions of their upbringing, the hypervigilance and constant desire for control that served them so well might manifest as persistent anxiety and an inability to relax. Their ability to recognise and manage their own emotional issues or to seek treatment when needed may be hindered by the very denial that has sheltered them from the harsh realities of addiction.

It's crucial to remember, though, that people who grew up in alcoholic homes are not merely the product of their environment. While they may be equipped with these traits and methods of coping, they are also incredibly powerful, resilient, and open to development. They can eventually unlearn maladaptive behaviours and establish healthier coping methods with the help of support, counselling, and introspection.

Redefining one's self-concept, confronting mistaken ideas, and learning healthy methods of relating to oneself and others are common components of healing and growth for those who grew up in alcoholic households. Having a group of people you can turn to for comfort, approval, and guidance as you learn to navigate relationships more effectively is a priceless asset.

People who grew up in alcoholic homes may be able to escape their environment and build a sober, successful life for themselves. They can heal, grow, and forge their own path beyond the limitations of their history if they acknowledge and deal with the effects of their upbringing.

Individuals who grew up in alcoholic homes may learn skills and traits that may aid them in their quest for wellness as they progress down their own paths to recovery and personal development.

The development of habits for caring for oneself is a crucial part of their healing process. Individuals who have struggled with addiction may understand the value of putting their own needs first. In order to care for their physical, mental, and emotional well-being, they may experiment with practices including mindfulness, exercise, creative outlets, and therapy. They can refuel, set healthy limits, and strengthen their feeling of self-worth by practicing self-care.

Learning effective ways to communicate is a critical part of their journey. It may be necessary for those who grew up in a hostile or ambiguous household to work on their ability to communicate clearly, openly, and compassionately. They may seek help from a therapist or attend a support group to learn how to communicate better, develop healthier relationships, and handle disagreements maturely.

People who grew up in alcoholic homes tend to place a premium on personal boundaries. Protecting their mental health and avoiding a recurrence of destructive relationships requires learning to establish and enforce healthy boundaries. They might figure out how to articulate their requirements, set boundaries, and explain their limitations to others. They establish a safe haven for mutual respect, self-care, and improved relationships through the use of boundaries.

Self-forgiveness and other-forgiveness are crucial components of the recovery process. People who grew up in alcoholic homes may have trouble letting go of grudges and blame, but as they heal, they may find the strength to do so. One's own development and the development of their relationships benefit from forgiveness since it releases them from the burden of the past and encourages them to adopt a more compassionate and self-accepting viewpoint.

Each person who grows up in an alcoholic home will have their own path to recovery. It calls for dedication, introspection, and the courage to face and overcome previous hurts. They may take back control of their lives and build a future full of resilience, purpose, and genuine connections by reflecting on their past, appreciating their strengths, and reaching out for help.

Chapter two

Going through your past

Having parents who drink heavily can have serious consequences for their children as they grow up. A person's adult emotional health, relationships, and development can all be influenced by their early life experiences and difficulties.

The emotional toll it takes on children is a major effect. Confusion, worry, and insecurity are common outcomes of a childhood marked by alcohol misuse. A child's sense of stability and trust in others might be damaged when they see their alcoholic parent's mood swings, anger, or neglect.

Alcoholism's disarray and turmoil can throw a family out of whack. Taking on adult responsibilities like child care and housework at a young age is common among children of alcoholic parents. They may feel overwhelmed and deprived of a carefree upbringing if they are expected to be responsible for others at a young age.

A child's perspective on relationships and coping mechanisms might be influenced by growing up in a household where alcohol is the primary focus. Maladaptive coping mechanisms for stress and emotions in children include isolation, people-pleasing, and the development of an unhealthy relationship with substances. These habits can follow a person into adulthood, making it difficult for them to make and keep friends, as well as deal with the stresses of daily life.

Children of alcoholics may have difficulty developing a healthy sense of self-worth and self-esteem. Feelings of guilt, shame, and self-blame can develop when children of alcoholics are exposed to their parent's unpredictable behaviour on a regular basis. They may start to feel guilty or defective themselves, blaming themselves for their parents' addiction. These distorted views of oneself might follow a person into adulthood, destroying his or her chances of success and pleasure.

The long-term repercussions of having parents who drank heavily might take many forms as an adult. To prevent themselves from feeling pain, some people may become overly cautious or avoidant. Some people may develop an unhealthy preference for partners whose personalities and interactions mirror those of their alcoholic parent.

It's important to remember, though, that not everyone who grows up with alcoholic parents ends up like their parents. Some people are able to strengthen their inner fortitude and perseverance via difficult circumstances, using those difficulties as stepping stones to greater maturity and compassion. They can overcome the difficulties of their upbringing through counselling, social networks, and introspection.

The long-term effects of having alcoholic parents are intricate and varied. Helping people recover from traumatic events in their youth and learn effective strategies for dealing with them is a complex process that calls for empathy, knowledge, and support.

People who had parents who drank excessively may have trouble controlling their own drinking as adults. Some people, after experiencing the negative effects of alcohol on themselves or their loved ones, may acquire a heightened sensitivity to it and decide to abstain from it altogether. Some people may be more vulnerable to substance misuse because they use it to self-medicate or to deal with emotional suffering that has not been addressed.

They may have trouble trusting others and developing close relationships because of emotional scars they suffered as children. As a result, they may have difficulty opening up to new people and maintaining existing friendships and relationships. They may subconsciously choose mates who mirror the dysfunctional habits they experienced as children, or they may develop a phobia of intimacy as a result.

Difficulties in personal and professional growth may stem from a lack of suitable role models and guidance during childhood. Education, career success, and happiness in life can all be hampered by a lack of consistent positive reinforcement and direction. Their inability to believe in themselves, make sound judgements, and establish appropriate limits might hinder both their personal and professional development.

Mental health problems are another consequence of having drunk parents. Anxiety, sadness, and other psychiatric problems have been linked to early life exposure to persistent stress and emotional instability. Therapy, counselling, or other interventions may be necessary to help overcome these difficulties by addressing traumatic experiences and fostering growth in coping mechanisms.

It's worth noting, though, that despite the risks, people raised by alcoholics sometimes show extraordinary resiliency and courage. They can create satisfying, healthy lives for themselves by receiving help, engaging in treatment, and developing personally.

Individuals can overcome their history, create healthy coping strategies, and build meaningful relationships by getting professional help, increasing self-awareness, and actively working on their emotional well-being. It can also be helpful to surround yourself with supportive friends, lovers, or support groups who have experienced similar things.

Society has a responsibility to those who have grown up with alcoholic parents by providing them with help, education, and support. Our efforts to educate the public, lessen the shame associated with substance abuse, and increase access to mental health care will help pave the way for adults who were impacted as children to obtain the resources they need to succeed as adults.

The repercussions of having parents who drink heavily can extend beyond an individual's own life. Without effective interventions, the cycle of addiction and dysfunction can continue to affect successive generations. The addiction cycle may be passed down through generations if children of alcoholics start abusing substances themselves.

Early intervention and support for families impacted by alcoholism is vital for breaking this cycle. Counselling, therapy, and support groups are all accessible and cost-effective options that can help parents overcome addiction, become better parents, and provide a healthier home life for their children. Parents can be motivated to get help and make positive adjustments if they are made aware of the negative effects their addiction has on their children.

The role of schools and other educational institutions in recognising and helping children from alcoholic families is crucial. Professionals like educators and counsellors can get the knowledge they need to spot the warning signs of abuse or neglect and respond appropriately. Helping children cope with their experiences and develop resilience can be facilitated by providing them with safe areas within schools to express their emotions and seek support.

Advocacy work such as public education campaigns and local efforts can also help reduce the stigma associated with substance abuse and increase public compassion. Society may encourage those who have been affected to seek treatment without feeling guilt or fear of judgement by spreading the tales of those who have overcome the difficulties of growing up with alcoholic parents.

Addiction treatment and mental health services should be given top priority in government policy and funding. Individuals and families impacted by alcoholism can heal and rebuild their lives with the support of accessible, low-cost therapy, counselling, and addiction treatment programmes. We can gain a deeper understanding of this problem and develop more useful therapies and support systems if we fund research on the long-term effects of having alcoholic parents.

Ultimately, it takes a diversified approach to break the cycle of addiction and lessen the impact of having alcoholic parents. It entails establishing policies that give priority to mental health and addiction treatment, as well as offering support and resources to individuals and families. By focusing on these aspects, we may work towards building a community that promotes the health and recovery of those who were raised by alcoholics.

How to unearth buried feelings, memories, and traumas

In many cases, the emotional wounds caused by having grown up with alcoholic parents go unnoticed and untreated. Alcoholism's erratic and discordant character can foster an atmosphere where feelings are repressed, memories are twisted, and traumas are buried.

Children with alcoholic parents typically develop resilience as a means of coping with the chaotic environment of their home. As a result of dealing with stress, conflict, and neglect on a regular basis, they may learn to adapt. Some individuals may numb their feelings, cut themselves off from their past, and up barriers to keep the hurt out.

As they age, some people may experience an increase in unexplainable emotional upheaval. It's possible they'll have outbursts of rage, depression, or loneliness. They don't realise that these feelings stem from childhood traumas and repressed memories.

Uncovering long-buried feelings, memories, and traumas can be an arduous and brave process. To do this, a safe and accepting environment must be created in which people may talk about their histories without worrying about being judged or stigmatised. Therapy or counselling from experts in dealing with trauma is typically part of this process.

Individuals can use the foundation of therapy to start peeling back the onion of their experiences. Therapists assist patients in unlocking long-forgotten memories by gently questioning and guiding them with empathy. They help establish a link between the feelings one is having at the moment and experiences from their upbringing.

As buried memories and feelings begin to surface, people may be forced to deal with a wide variety of feelings they've been avoiding or denying for a long time. Because of the neglect and instability they experienced, kids may be angry with their parents. They may feel a sense of loss for the lack of a safe and caring environment in which to grow up. For having such unfavourable feelings towards their parents, they may feel guilty and ashamed.

Recognising and accepting these feelings as reasonable reactions to past events is an important part of the healing process. To heal, one must master the ability to forgive oneself and others. The key to ending the cycle of dysfunction is learning appropriate coping techniques for dealing with difficult feelings and controlling one's responses.

Individuals can learn how their childhood has influenced their values, habits, and interactions with others through introspection and counselling. They are able to recognise habits that they have repeated unknowingly and actively make decisions to change them.

Even while it may hurt, digging up long-buried feelings, memories, and traumas can lead to personal development and change. It enables people to regain control of their lives, discover new dimensions of themselves, and build more satisfying connections with others. They can move forward into a better, more fulfilled future by facing their previous hurts head-on.

Healing times may vary from person to person because of how highly individualised this process is. The process of discovering and healing from repressed feelings, memories, and traumas associated with being raised by alcoholic parents requires patience, self-compassion, and continual assistance.

Unexpected obstacles and insights may be encountered as people continue their journey of uncovering repressed feelings, memories, and traumas from growing up with alcoholic parents. As they peel back each layer, they discover new information that aids in their recovery.

The effects of parental drunkenness on their own feeling of value and pride are something that regularly comes up. Children whose parents' addictions made it difficult for them to get the attention and care they needed as children often develop negative views of themselves. They may have convinced themselves that they are not deserving of a caring community or the help of others.

Negative self-perceptions can be addressed by actively confronting and reframing them. Self-compassion, self-care, and self-validation are all part of the process. In therapy, people can learn to value themselves for who they truly are and grow in independence from their dysfunctional background.

When recovering from the effects of growing up with alcoholic parents, it's important to go back and face the unpleasant experiences you may have pushed aside or fractured. Abuse, either physical or emotional, neglect, or exposure to threatening behaviour all fit under this category. People can feel a wide range of emotions, from fear to despair to numbness, as these memories emerge.

The safe space provided by a therapist makes it possible to go through the emotions linked with these traumatic events. Based on the patient's specific requirements, they may use a variety of approaches, such as cognitive behavioural therapy, EMDR (Eye Movement Desensitisation and Reprocessing), or somatic experience. These techniques help people piece together their traumatic experiences into a narrative that makes sense, which in turn promotes closure and recovery.

Simultaneously, people may investigate how their upbringing has shaped their interpersonal dynamics and the relationships they've formed. Having an alcoholic parent or other family member can have a negative impact on a child's ability to form positive attachments and learn effective coping mechanisms. Trust, relationships, and communication can all suffer as a result.

By being aware of them, people can make deliberate changes to escape toxic relationship dynamics. They can learn more positive approaches to relationship development, boundary setting, and communication. They learn how their histories have shaped their current connections with one another through counselling. This insight equips people to make deliberate adjustments, leading to improved health and more satisfying connections with others.

Liberation and a renewed sense of agency are common outcomes of the healing process. They are free from the burden of repressed feelings and unresolved pain. Instead, they accept their weaknesses, acknowledge their feelings, and act truthfully.

It is not a straight line from having alcoholic parents to working with repressed feelings, memories, and traumas. It has its ups and downs, its lucid and hazy patches. However, as time passes, people are able to recover their lives and create new histories for themselves.

Keep in mind that recovery is a continuous procedure. Sometimes, even after a lot of progress, something will happen to set you back. Newfound resilience and coping mechanisms, however, equip people to overcome these setbacks and advance on the road to psychological health and development.

By bringing to the surface long-buried feelings, experiences, and traumas, people are able to break free from their past and build a future based on healing, self-love, and resilience.

People who were raised by alcoholics typically learn the value of self-care and alternative healing methods as they go through their own repressed emotions, memories, and traumas. They have come to understand that taking care of their emotional, mental, and spiritual health is just as important as attending treatment sessions.

The importance of maintaining a healthy body cannot be overstated. They realise that taking care of one's physique can have a beneficial effect on one's mental and emotional health. Regular exercise, a healthy diet, and enough of sleep all contribute to someone's health and happiness. They develop habits of self-care that foster restoration and fortitude by tuning in to their body' cues about what it needs.

Their mental health is also a top priority as they recover. They learn to fight for their own mental health and actively seek out methods of coping with stress, anxiety, and the aftereffects of traumatic situations. They investigate techniques like meditation and mindfulness that can help them become more in tune with the here and now and with their own selves. They may also find solace and release via artistic pursuits like writing, painting, or music.

Also helpful for those on the road to recovery is making connections with those who understand what they're going through. They can find legitimacy for their experiences and sympathy from people who can relate thanks to support groups or online forums for people who grew up with alcoholic parents. Participating in a group that understands and encourages their process of recovery can do wonders for their progress.

They may also find that investigating their spirituality is crucial to their recovery. They can be on the lookout for a way to get in touch with their true selves and a greater power. Meditation, prayer, and time spent in nature are all good options for this kind of introspective digging. It helps individuals find comfort, meaning, and the ability to rise beyond their suffering.

The ability to forgive may also undergo radical transformation during the healing process. Releasing oneself from the emotional weight of bitterness and hatred is what forgiveness of alcoholic parents actually accomplishes. It's a decision they make for themselves that lets them stop worrying about what their parents will do and start prioritising their own happiness.

When a person is raised by alcoholics, they may bury their feelings, memories, and traumas, but the process of discovering them can lead to profound growth and change. Self-actualization entails regaining one's true identity, mending emotional scars, and constructing a happy, healthy existence.

As people keep going down this road, they prove the world that healing and resiliency are real. They may decide to help others by telling their own recovery stories, raising awareness about mental health and substance abuse, or encouraging those who are also in recovery. Those who are still looking for their own route to emotional health and wholeness will find encouragement and guidance in their stories.

It is never too late to rewrite our stories and create a life of purpose, fulfilment, and emotional well-being; the journey of uncovering repressed emotions, memories, and traumas becomes a testament to the strength of the human spirit and the capacity for healing and growth.

Therapeutic methods

Growth, insight, and comprehension of oneself are all possible outcomes of the reflective and introspective processes of self-reflection and -introspection. Several therapeutic approaches and instruments have been developed to aid people in exploring their inner worlds of feelings, memories, and experiences. These methods inspire introspection, epiphany, and change by facilitating contact with one's inner world.

Journaling is one of the most basic methods of introspection. Writing is a kind of communication that allows people to open up about their innermost ideas, feelings, and experiences. Writing in a journal can be a kind of therapeutic self-exploration because it removes the threat of being judged. It helps people see things more plainly, recognize patterns, and draw links between previously unrelated events. An individual's path of self-discovery can be charted, goals established, and lessons learned via frequent journal writing.

The practice of mindfulness meditation is another helpful method for introspection. Mindfulness training helps people become objective observers of their inner mental and emotional experiences. This method fosters being in the here and now and invites people to openly and honestly investigate their own subjective experiences. With the insight gained via mindfulness meditation, people are better able to deal with the ups and downs of daily life.

Another method that can encourage introspection is art therapy. People's inner worlds can be discovered and explored via the use of many artistic techniques. Art therapy is a powerful tool because it allows patients to communicate nonverbally and access their inner world. Individuals can get insight into their own minds and hearts through the creative process by tapping into long-repressed feelings, experiences, and convictions. Art therapy is a therapeutic approach that uses creative methods to help people explore and appreciate their unique selves.

The process of introspection can be greatly aided by talking things through with a therapist or other reliable people. Individuals can expand their worldviews, have their beliefs tested, and learn more about themselves through having meaningful conversations with others. Skilled therapists can help their patients gain insight into themselves by asking probing questions and creating a safe space for introspection. The ability to share one's thoughts with another and accept constructive criticism is a powerful tool for self-exploration.

Visualization and mind mapping are two further tools that might help with introspection. Mind maps are diagrams that help you map out your ideas, connections, and thoughts visually. A mind map is a visual representation of ideas that helps its creator see patterns, draw conclusions, and focus on what needs more consideration.

Guided imagery, sometimes known as "mental journeys," is one form of visualization that helps people form concrete mental representations of their goals, aspirations, and experiences. Using visualization, one can have a more profound comprehension of one's own aspirations, drives, and inner resources.

You can improve your capacity for introspection and self-analysis by consulting self-help materials like books, podcasts, and websites. These materials provide helpful information, models, and activities for introspection. Emotional intelligence, self-compassion, resilience, and finding one's life's purpose are just few of the areas in which they might be helpful. Using these materials can lead to the development of novel concepts, the promotion of introspection, and the provision of a framework for future thought.

Chapter three

The Effects of Alcoholism

Alcoholism is characterized by the fact that it worsens over time. The problem usually begins with social or moderate drinking and progresses to an unhealthy reliance on alcohol to manage emotional distress or other difficulties. This slow but steady increase usually results in tolerance, when more and more alcohol is needed to obtain the same effects.

When alcoholics try to cut back on or stop drinking, they experience withdrawal symptoms. Tremors, anxiety, nausea, insomnia, and even hallucinations are all examples of symptoms that can range from being somewhat annoying to being extremely distressing. People may keep drinking to avoid or dull the pain of these events, which might contribute to the maintenance of alcohol consumption.

Genetic, physiological, and environmental aspects are all considered in the illness model of alcoholism. There may be a hereditary susceptibility to alcoholism, as studies have indicated that certain people have a genetic tendency to drinking. Furthermore, specific neurochemical abnormalities in the brain have been discovered in people with alcoholism, particularly affecting dopamine and serotonin, lending further credence to the disease hypothesis.

Alcoholism has far-reaching consequences that touch more than just physical health. In addition to raising the risk for mood disorders like melancholy and anxiety, alcohol consumption has been linked to impairments in thinking and memory. Because the person's attention and energy are diverted to getting and using alcohol, this might cause problems in their personal and professional relationships.

Alcoholism treatment plans should take into account both the physiological and psychosocial elements of the disorder. The first phase is usually detoxification, which helps the body get rid of the alcohol while the withdrawal symptoms are being managed. Detoxification is only the first step towards recovery from alcoholism; further rehabilitation programmes such as counselling, therapy, and support groups are essential for identifying and addressing the underlying causes of alcohol abuse.

Rather than seeing alcoholism as a moral failing or a lack of willpower, it's crucial to view it as a chronic condition that requires compassion and understanding. Admitting that alcoholism is a disease helps to normalise the condition, lessens the negative connotations associated with it, and guarantees that those who suffer from it will get the help they need to recover.

The physical health of an alcoholic is another important factor to consider. Liver disease, cardiovascular problems, pancreatitis, gastrointestinal troubles, and a compromised immune system are just some of the many health concerns that can result from chronic and excessive alcohol usage. These medical issues have the potential to be extremely harmful, even fatal. Further endangering the individual's health is the fact that excessive alcohol consumption raises the likelihood of accidents, injuries, and participation in risky behaviours.

Alcoholism has significant monetary and societal costs. The illness can lead to lost work, unstable finances, legal problems, and poor relationships at home. Because of their obsession with alcohol and the changes in their behaviour, the person may find it difficult to maintain relationships with those closest to them. Isolation, along with the stigma and guilt that surround alcoholism, can have a devastating effect on a person's mental health, amplifying their emotions of helplessness and despair.

Understanding the complex interplay of causes is essential for designing effective interventions for alcohol use disorders. A person's ability to regulate or cease drinking decreases with time because to the disease's progressive nature, even if the choice to drink initially was voluntary. This inability to refrain from drinking is what distinguishes alcoholism from simple binge drinking.

Fortunately, advances in alcoholism therapy over the years have given alcoholics hope for a full recovery. In addition to professional medical help and therapy, support organisations like Alcoholics Anonymous (AA) can help people who are trying to overcome their alcoholism by putting them in touch with others who are going through the same things they are.

The fight against alcoholism also benefits greatly from prevention and education efforts. We can lessen the prevalence and societal effect of this disease by increasing public understanding of the dangers of alcohol addiction, enacting legislation to control the availability and use of alcohol, and creating a welcoming and accepting atmosphere for those struggling with alcoholism.

Alcoholism's effects are felt well beyond the individual and have profound repercussions for society as a whole. Healthcare, lost productivity, and the legal system all contribute to alcoholism's hefty price tag. Alcoholism has far-reaching consequences, impacting all spheres of society through decreased productivity, increased healthcare costs, and increased crime and violence.

It is especially dangerous for children to grow up in alcoholic homes. Neglect, abuse, and instability are all things that children may face, all of which can have devastating repercussions on their mental, emotional, and physical health. Children of alcoholics have an increased risk of becoming alcoholics themselves, so continuing the generational cycle of drinking.

It takes more than just personal effort to recover from alcoholism; a supportive community and enough resources are also crucial. It is the responsibility of society as a whole to ensure that those who are battling with alcoholism have access to information, destigmatization, and treatment. Supportive communities that encourage healthy coping skills and alternatives to alcohol are crucial, as are early intervention and prevention programmes.

Addiction recovery is a lifelong process that calls for constant dedication and encouragement. Adopting a healthy lifestyle, surrounding oneself with positive people, and learning to cope well are all important components of long-term sobriety. Relapse is a reality, but with the right support system in place, those who have struggled with alcoholism can learn to control their disease and live productive lives.

The emotional, psychological, and physiological ways that alcoholism can affect a family

There are several physical problems that might arise when drinking is present in a family. High levels of stress are common among people who live with alcoholics due to the unpredictability of the alcoholic's behaviour and environment. Headaches, muscle tightness, gastrointestinal issues, and inability to sleep are just some of the physical manifestations of chronic stress and tension. Because of the demands of caring for an alcoholic, family members may find it difficult to prioritise their own health and happiness.

Alcoholism may wreak havoc on a family's emotional stability. Emotional ups and downs, such as rage, irritation, grief, fear, and helplessness, are common for those close to us. They may harbour resentment against the alcoholic because of the alcoholic's actions and the toll it takes on their relationships. Because of the unpredictability of the circumstance, family members may become hypervigilant, living on edge and ready for any crisis that may arise. The family may feel ashamed or embarrassed to talk to others about their problems, which can increase the sense of isolation they have.

The mental health of loved ones is severely damaged by alcoholism. Living in such a volatile and uncertain setting can cause anxiety and sadness. Because they may grow to blame themselves for the alcoholic's condition or feel powerless to aid the alcoholic in breaking their addiction, the ongoing stress and emotional strain can destroy their self-esteem and confidence, leaving them feeling inadequate or guilty. These mental repercussions can, in time, cause one to feel like one has lost one's individuality and is confined inside the confines of one's own family structure.

Family members who drink too much might sabotage normal lines of communication. Fear of confrontation or retaliation can prevent open and honest communication within families, leading individuals to repress their feelings and put off confronting the problem. The stigma and isolation that surround alcoholism can make it hard for loved ones to reach out for help or talk about their experiences. When family members have trouble communicating with one another, it can add to their sense of isolation and make it harder for them to get the care they need.

The effects of drinking on children in the home are substantial. There is a risk of routine disruption, erratic parenting, and a dearth of emotional support for the child. As a result, they may have trouble forming healthy relationships, struggle in school, and perhaps develop an addiction to harmful substances later in life.

Alcoholism can have far-reaching and enduring consequences for family relationships. Trust, the cornerstone of any strong relationship, is often damaged in an alcoholic household. Trust between family members is eroded when they constantly break promises, tell lies, and cross boundaries. This loss of faith can put a severe strain on family ties, leading to schisms amongst spouses, siblings, parents, and children.

Alterations in family role dynamics are also possible. Those closest to an alcoholic may find themselves playing unexpected positions, such as carer or facilitator. One or a select few family members may end up shouldering the bulk of dealing with the fallout from an alcoholic's actions, which can cause anger and an unfair distribution of responsibilities. These shifts in responsibility might alter the dynamic of authority within the household.

Another common effect of drinking on loved ones is financial stress. Addiction may be quite expensive for families because of things like buying alcohol, having to go to the hospital, paying for legal help, and possibly losing a job. When money is spent on dealing with the effects of alcoholism instead of meeting fundamental requirements or pursuing personal ambitions, it can lead to stress, anxiety, and even poverty.

Growing up in an alcoholic home can be difficult for children. A lack of regularity and predictability in their lives may cause them anxiety and concern about the future. When children are exposed to or experience verbal, physical, or emotional abuse at home, it can have a profound effect on their mental health. Negative effects on their sense of self-worth, relationships, and general well-being may persist into adulthood as a result.

The effects of drinking on future generations are equally important. There is a correlation between growing up in an alcoholic home and subsequently struggling with substance misuse problems. They may internalise the norms and practises they saw their parents engage in, contributing to a generational cycle of substance abuse. Intentional intervention and assistance that addresses not only the addiction but also the underlying family relationships and traumas is necessary for breaking away from this cycle.

Recognising the layered complexity of alcoholism's affects on loved ones is crucial. There could be a wide range of responses and outcomes because of the unique perspectives and experiences of each member of the family. The alcoholic and their loved ones can benefit greatly from seeking professional help in the form of counselling or support groups in order to cope with the difficulties associated with alcoholism and to facilitate healing and recovery.

Family members' alcoholism can have far-reaching consequences, affecting not just the alcoholic's immediate family but also their acquaintances and neighbours. Family and social engagements may become tense as loved ones try to figure out how to deal with the alcoholic's drinking or their behaviour. Family members may withdraw from social activities or feel criticised and misunderstood by those who are ignorant of the difficulties they experience, which can put a strain on relationships and contribute to feelings of isolation.

Personal ambitions and aspirations may get pushed aside while family members struggle with the aftereffects of alcoholism. Addiction's after-effects can drain a person of time, motivation, and resources, making it difficult for them to advance their education, job, or personal development. Frustration, unrealized potential, and hatred towards the alcoholic may result.

There's a chance that family members will lose hope, too. Seeing the damaging effects of drinking and the difficulties of rehabilitation might dampen hopes for a brighter tomorrow. As a result, family members may feel helpless and resigned, unable to see a future in which their loved one is no longer enslaved by addiction.

Despite the many obstacles and struggles, family members can be an integral part of the healing process. They can help the alcoholic heal and change for the better if they get help for themselves and push them towards treatment. All members of the family will feel more secure and supported if there is an atmosphere of empathy, understanding, and firm boundaries.

Chapter four

How codependency works and how it facilitates addictive behavior

Codependency is a difficult-to-break destructive cycle since it is a multifaceted psychological pattern that frequently intertwines with addictive behaviours. Codependency is characterised by an unhealthy reliance on others for feelings of worth, approval, and identification. People with codependent tendencies are more likely to be in relationships where they put the emotional needs of their partners ahead of their own.

Codependency is a major factor in the development and maintenance of addictive behaviours. Codependency develops when an individual's sense of self-worth is intertwined with that of the addicted person, who is often a loved one. One possible response is to act as a caretaker, attempting to protect the addict from the inevitable outcomes of their drug use.

The empathy and want to help others displayed by many codependents is twisted by their own addiction. Because of a misplaced idea that they are protecting the addict or maintaining the connection, they may support the addict out of a deep-seated fear of abandonment or rejection. Addiction enablement can take the form of monetary assistance, justification of the addict's behaviour, or a refusal to address the problem.

Codependence is often accompanied by a lack of ability to establish and keep healthy limits. When they put their own needs ahead of the addict's, they struggle to say "no" and experience shame as a result. The lack of limits and the consequent lack of repercussions for the addict's actions only serve to strengthen the codependency between them.

The codependent's sense of worth is often tied to the addict's perception of it. Addicts and their loved ones often create an unhealthy sense of responsibility, thinking that only they have the ability to change the addict's behaviour and save them from destruction. The codependent's warped belief system keeps them trapped in the addictive cycle, as they look to their role as saviour for affirmation and meaning.

Codependency can obstruct the addict's and the codependent's path to recovery. Because of their fixation on the addict's needs, codependents often neglect their own problems and fears. By avoiding their own emotional development, enablers reinforce the addictive behaviour of those they help.

Recovering from codependency is a challenging process that calls for introspection, treatment, and community. Self-respect involves appreciating one's own value and setting appropriate limits. Realising that one can't change or cure someone else's addiction and that change must come from within is equally essential.

As a conclusion, codependency is linked to addictive behaviours because it promotes a destructive cycle of enabling and rescuing. Lack of boundaries and self-neglect by the codependent keep the addiction going, feeding the codependent's need for affirmation and fear of abandonment. Both the codependent and the addict must break out of their codependency if they are to achieve long-term sobriety and mental health.

The mental and emotional well-being of the codependent person may also suffer as a result of their codependency. As they put the addict's demands ahead of their own, they may stop taking care of themselves, bury their feelings, and give up on their own ambitions. Neglecting oneself in this way can result in bitterness, anger, and an overwhelming sense of loneliness.

Hope and disillusionment are common emotions for those who are codependent. When the addict shows improvement or makes vows to change, the loved one may feel hopeful, only to be disappointed when the addictive behaviour returns. The codependent's sense of responsibility for the addict's welfare is bolstered by this pattern, and their will to "fix" the problem is strengthened.

Codependency can keep the codependent and the addict feeling helpless. The codependent may become preoccupied with trying to manage the addict's actions that they forget to take care of themselves. Meanwhile, the addict could lean on the codependent for comfort instead of facing their addiction head-on and getting assistance.

Communication problems and a lack of emotional closeness are common in codependent relationships. As long as the addict's addiction and the codependent's caring role are front and centre, it can be difficult for both parties to communicate their genuine feelings and needs. Because of the inability to connect on a deeper level, both parties may experience increased emotions of loneliness and resentment.

It is essential for the codependent to start on a journey of self-discovery and self-care in order to break free from codependency and address the enabling of addictive behaviours. To do so, one must learn to value oneself, identify one's own wants and needs, and set and stick to appropriate limits with others.

Counselling and peer support groups can be helpful resources during rehabilitation. Codependents can develop healthier coping techniques and gain insight into the origins of their codependency through treatment. Individuals can feel less alone in their recovery process when they join a support group and talk to others who understand what they're going through.

Independent of the addict's decisions, the codependent must prioritise their own recovery and development. This may entail establishing boundaries around their engagement with the addict's life, pursuing interests outside of the addict's, and building relationships with people who can offer healthy emotional support.

Self-awareness, self-compassion, and personal development are essential for overcoming codependency and the addictive behaviours it facilitates. For both the codependent and the addict, this is a difficult process that calls for time, patience, and support, but it can lead to better relationships, greater personal fulfilment, and greater emotional well-being.

It is crucial for the codependent person to strengthen their sense of self and practise self-care on the path to overcoming codependency and enabling addictive behaviours. This is caring for themselves in a way that is unrelated to the addict, which includes getting in touch with their own feelings, desires, and values.

A few examples of self-care practises are doing things that make you happy, making time for rest and introspection, and putting your physical and mental health first. Codependents can start recovering from their condition by prioritising their own needs and happiness.

The healing process is aided by the acquisition of constructive communication skills. Those who struggle with codependency would do well to practise assertiveness, learn to communicate their needs and feelings in a healthy way, and cultivate the ability to actively listen to others without compromising their own limits.

Involving the addict in his or her own recovery might help them both personally and professionally. Addiction treatment programmes, peer support groups, and professional help can arm the addict with the resources they need to overcome their habit. The codependent must accept that they have no power over the addict's rehabilitation, but that they may provide support by promoting good decisions and setting limits.

It is also important to rebuild and fortify the codependent's social support system. Validation, encouragement, and a sense of belonging can all be gained by surrounding oneself with people who understand and support one's recovery process. Codependency support groups provide a secure place for people to talk to others who understand what they're going through and offer advice based on their own experiences.

Chapter five

Ending the Cycle

One of the most important things you can do for your own development, happiness, and success in life is to break away from destructive habits and routines. These tend to be habitual ways of behaving that have a powerful impact on how we feel and what we do. They prevent us from developing meaningful connections with others, achieving our ambitions, and finding true joy in life.

Negativity and unhappiness tend to be maintained through dysfunctional routines, which is why breaking free from them is so important. Whether it's partaking in bad behaviours, staying in unhealthy relationships, or adhering to false beliefs, repeating these patterns keeps us mired in a downward spiral of unhappiness. To break free is to accept that we can transform our current situation and to actively seek out more beneficial alternatives that will allow us to develop and achieve our full potential.

Unhealed emotional scars and traumatic experiences from the past are common sources of dysfunctional habits. These habits may have helped us manage stressful situations in the past, but they now get in the way of our development. Once we are able to separate ourselves from these shackles, we may finally face and heal the emotional scars that have been keeping us back. Through introspection and healing, we can strengthen our sense of identity, boost our confidence, and develop our capacity for kindness towards ourselves.

Dysfunctional patterns and behaviours can also have a devastating effect on the quality of our interpersonal connections. Conflict and discontent can easily become a vicious cycle when one partner engages in dysfunctional behaviours such as poor communication, codependence, or an avoidance of intimacy. When we are able to break out of these routines, we can build stronger relationships with others. It enables us to set limits, have fruitful exchanges, and selectively form bonds with people who value and support us emotionally and intellectually.

When we remove ourselves from destructive routines, we also reassume control over our own destinies. It entails realising that we control our own destinies and outcomes, regardless of our current situation. When we break free from these habits, we create space for personal development, expansion, and more agency. We stop being bystanders in our own lives and start taking an active role in shaping them.

On the road to recovery from destructive habits and routines, we come upon the chance to reinvent ourselves and build a world that better reflects who we truly are. This process calls for bravery, introspection, and a determination to better oneself.

The ability to question and confront long-held assumptions is crucial to achieving independence. These views could have been influenced by things like cultural norms, psychological trauma, or adverse life experiences. We can, however, discover their flaws with a critical eye and make a conscious decision to replace them with new, empowering ideas.

In order to liberate ourselves from destructive habits, we must also examine our feelings and identify the motivating factors that drive our actions. To do so, we must cultivate emotional intelligence and learn to manage our emotions effectively. With the help of this introspection, we can develop a kinder and more accepting attitude towards ourselves and others.

The road to independence is fraught with challenges and setbacks, so keep that in mind as you travel. It's possible you'll face obstacles, encounter times of resistance, and feel tempted to fall back on old habits. Perseverance and a dedication to improvement, however, will allow us to go over these obstacles and into the future.

Leaving behind destructive routines makes room for self-reinvention and the pursuit of new opportunities. It frees our minds to explore new possibilities, allowing us to develop our interests, skills, and abilities. When we release our inhibitions, we become free to become a more complete version of ourselves and to seek a life that is full of depth and meaning.

Inspiring and influencing those around us is another benefit of breaking free from unhealthy routines. By setting an example of positive actions, genuineness, and personal growth, we can help those around us who are also seeking change. The beneficial effects of our personal development can extend beyond ourselves and permeate our social networks and the places we call home.

Self-liberation occurs when one finally succeeds in overcoming harmful habits and routines. It's about accepting and appreciating who we really are and deciding how we want to live our lives. It calls for introspection, adaptability, and a dedication to continuous development. As we progress down this path of self-discovery, we open the door to radical self-development and the birth of a life that is genuine, satisfying, and in harmony with our deepest wishes.

As we move forward on the path of release from dysfunctional patterns and behaviours, we get a sense of freedom and growth in various areas of our lives. Our increased independence empowers us to act in accordance with our values and goals rather than reacting automatically to situations or giving in to peer pressure.

The regaining of pride in oneself is a priceless benefit of achieving independence. Confidence is lost, and a sense of helplessness and helplessness is a common result of repeating dysfunctional habits. However, as we break free from these routines, we realise our own value and grow in confidence. We reject our inability to learn from our mistakes or expand beyond our current circumstances and instead celebrate our infinite potential.

After you've broken free from dysfunctional patterns, you'll find a whole new world of opportunities for development and improvement. It forces us to expand our horizons and try something new. The more we learn, explore, and broaden our perspectives, the more curious we become. This development feeds our minds, enlarges our horizons, and deepens our comprehension of who we are and the world around us.

Freedom also helps you become more resilient and flexible. The more habits we are able to let go of, the more prepared we will be to deal with the inevitable difficulties and unknowns that life brings. Strength of character and the ability to recover quickly from adversity are cultivated in us. Because of this capacity for resilience, we are able to view life's difficulties less as insurmountable obstacles and more as possibilities for personal development.

Freeing ourselves from destructive habits also has far-reaching effects on our interpersonal connections. We make room for genuine friendships based on mutual respect, trust, and emotional well-being when we let go of destructive patterns and habits. Understanding our own limits and needs improves our ability to communicate with others, establish reasonable expectations, and create true connections with those around us. The people in our lives no longer cause us pain or dysfunction but instead provide us with support, progress, and a sense of fulfilment.

Freeing ourselves from destructive habits gives us the agency to choose a life that matters. With this newfound independence, we are better able to live our lives in accordance with our deepest convictions, pursue meaningful occupations, and make meaningful contributions to the world. Living an honest and purposeful life has a ripple effect that benefits those around us.

Chapter six

The importance of setting limits with alcoholic parents

For one's own well-being and development, setting good boundaries with alcoholic parents is crucial. A person's life can be turned upside down when their parent is an alcoholic, and they may feel a wide range of bad feelings as a result. In order to protect their mental and emotional health, preserve their individuality, and cultivate healthy connections, it becomes crucial for them to set firm limits.

To begin, people can safeguard their own safety by establishing limits for themselves. Having to deal with drunk parents can be stressful and nerve-wracking. The possibility for verbal or physical abuse, as well as unstable behaviour, might have serious psychological consequences. By establishing limits, children can protect their developing identities and sense of self from their parents' influence. This time apart allows people to concentrate on their own needs, reach out for help, and partake in activities that boost their mental health.

Setting limits also aids in protecting one's sense of self and moral compass. The disarray and disorder brought on by parental alcoholism can make it difficult to distinguish between one's own wants and needs and those of one's parents. Without limits, children and other loved ones may give up on their own lives in an effort to help their addicted parents. By establishing reasonable limits, they show they are committed to their own growth, development, and pursuit of pleasure, so affirming their own ideals and objectives.

Relationships with alcoholic parents improve when children establish limits with their parents. Codependency develops when children of alcoholics assume responsibility for their parents' drinking or mental health. However, this dynamic can't last because it serves no one's best interests. One way to help parents learn to take responsibility for their own behaviours and decisions is to help their children create healthy boundaries with them. This provides an opening for the parents to get sober themselves by getting the treatment they need to deal with their addiction. Furthermore, having clear limits encourages honest and open dialogue, leading to a more balanced, respectful, and supportive partnership.

It might be difficult to set boundaries with alcoholic parents because doing so typically involves facing one's own anxieties, guilt, and codependent tendencies. Boundaries can be both physical, such as a curfew or visiting hours, and emotional, such as a refusal to accept verbal abuse or enable destructive behaviour. It can be quite helpful to seek out professional help like counselling or support groups as you make your way through this trying time.

Self-respect and safety demand the bravery of setting boundaries with alcoholic parents. It enables people to safeguard their mental and emotional health, hold fast to their own principles, and foster more satisfying interpersonal connections. Setting healthy boundaries allows people to end destructive patterns and open up opportunities for development, healing, and contentment in their lives.

Setting good boundaries with alcoholic parents can have significant effects on family dynamics in addition to the individual benefits. When members of a family set limits for one another, it creates a structure for more positive interactions between members. If there are younger siblings or other family members involved, this can provide a more secure and stable setting for everyone.

Setting limits on what's allowed and what isn't aids in establishing order and regularity in one's life. This can be especially helpful for kids and teens who are living in an alcoholic home since it helps them feel grounded and normal despite their circumstances. As a bonus, modelling healthy relationship dynamics teaches kids the value of respecting oneself, speaking up for oneself, and setting limits.

Setting limits can help the alcoholic parent take responsibility for his or her actions. When people make it plain what they will and will not tolerate from others, they send a strong message. This may serve as a wake-up call for the parent, making them face the real-world repercussions of their addiction and encouraging them to get assistance or make some changes.

Setting limits does not ensure the alcoholic parent will stop drinking or suddenly modify their behaviour, but it can help. Alcoholism is a difficult disease that calls for expert care and a strong personal resolve to overcome. Setting limits can help improve family relationships, but it's important to remember that no one has the power to change or cure their parent's addiction.

If the alcoholic parent's behaviour continues to be hurtful or detrimental, the individual may need to set more rigid boundaries, such as limiting or cutting off contact. This is a tough decision that must be made in the sake of one's own physical and emotional well-being.

Learning to create boundaries with alcoholic parents is a path to personal development and recovery. It enables people to reclaim control of their lives, develop more positive connections with others, and make their homes safer places to live. By establishing limits for themselves, people may demonstrate their value, put their health and happiness first, and create the road for a more positive and self-determined future.

Setting good boundaries with alcoholic parents is a process, and individuals may experience a range of emotions as they do so. Recognise that this is not a straight line, and expect obstacles and setbacks along the way. Individuals can keep their personal well-being as a top priority and keep their boundaries in place if they are persistent and kind to themselves.

Guilt or a feeling of responsibility for one's parents' addiction is one obstacle that some people must overcome. It is typical for children to internalise their parents' problems and attribute them to themselves. But it's important to keep in mind that addiction is a complicated condition that can't be attributed to anything else. When children establish limits with their parents, they are not giving up on or betraying them. Rather, they are protecting themselves and fostering healthier dynamics in the family unit as a whole.

Setting limits with alcoholic parents might also be met with resistance or opposition. Maintaining one's limits while showing compassion and sympathy for the difficulties the parent may be through is crucial. An increased awareness and respect for one's demands and limits might result from the calm, firm expression of such boundaries. Setting limits that are overly hard or unreachable may lead to extra tension or strain in the relationship, so it's important to strike a balance.

Having reliable friends, family, and/or experts to lean on throughout this process can be really helpful. You can find a safe place to work through your feelings, gain some perspective, and get some advice on how to handle tough situations by joining a support group for people whose lives have been damaged by alcoholism or by going to counselling. Talking to people who have been in similar situations can help provide validation, support, and tangible ideas for setting and keeping good boundaries.

Remember that your purpose in establishing limits is not to manipulate or change your alcoholic parent. It is up to each person to make their own decisions and to find their own path to wellness. The goal should be to foster development and well-being in oneself by establishing a better and more long-lasting dynamic.

Lovingly separating from alcoholic

Lovingly separating from alcoholic parents can be difficult, but it may be the first step towards a healthy life for you. Some tips to assist you find your way through this and build a community of support are provided below.

First, realising that separating with love entails taking care of yourself and establishing healthy boundaries with your parents is essential. You must accept that you are powerless to stop their addiction and that it is not your fault that they are addicted. To proceed, it is essential that you accept this truth.

Putting your own mental and physical health first is an act of loving detachment. Do things that make you happy and give you a sense of accomplishment as a means of self-care. Activities like hobby-seeking, self-care, and development-oriented thinking fall into this category. Keep in mind the importance of prioritising your own happiness and well-being.

During this time, it is crucial to establish a network of support. Find people who can relate to your predicament and offer support and advice. Get in touch with people who have been through the addiction process themselves and can listen to your feelings without judgement. Participating in therapy or counselling can also be helpful since it provides an outside, objective viewpoint that can guide you as you learn to manage your feelings and move forward.

It's crucial to strengthen one's sense of identity and foster inner resilience in addition to relying on others for help. Methods that help with this include keeping a journal and being mindful. Put your energy into discovering who you are as an individual, without the influence of your parents' addiction.

Feelings of remorse, wrath, and despair are normal companions on this path. Allow yourself to feel these emotions without shame or guilt, and think about getting professional help to go through them.

Remember that lovingly detaching does not imply abandoning your parents. The key is to set up reasonable limits that will keep you safe without stifling any future possibilities for development or alteration. Addiction is a serious problem, and getting sober is a process that might vary from person to person and take some time.

Lovingly detaching from alcoholic parents is difficult, but it's possible to establish a happier, more satisfying life for yourself by focusing on your own needs, surrounding yourself with positive people, and practising self-compassion. It takes strength to ask for assistance, but know that you are not alone.

Be ready for probable setbacks and hardships as you continue on your road of detaching with love and creating a support network. Your parents' battle with addiction is complicated and ongoing; they may relapse or refuse help. Keeping your boundaries in place and putting your own needs first is especially important now.

Be confident and forceful when talking to your parents. Maintaining a respectful and caring tone when expressing your wants, concerns, and boundaries is essential. Keep in mind that you are only responsible for your own reactions, not theirs. Maintain strict limits, and don't engage in any enabling behaviour that could help feed their addiction.

As you distance yourself, it can be beneficial to participate in pursuits that help you learn more about yourself and improve as a person. This could mean starting a new hobby, going back to school, or starting a side project. By investing in yourself, you're taking the initiative to create a rewarding life outside of addiction.

The task of establishing a solid network of allies is never complete. You may look into counselling programmes that focus on family dynamics and addiction, or you could join a support group for adult children of alcoholics. These communities can be a source of encouragement, understanding, and helpful advice from those who have been where you are.

Taking time for self-care to improve your physical, emotional, and mental health is just as important as reaching out to others for assistance. Get plenty of exercise, healthy food, and shut-eye on a regular basis. Try some deep breathing exercises, yoga, or meditation to calm your mind and find some inner peace.

Keep in mind that there is more to establishing a network of support than simply asking for help. Having a strong network of people who care about your development and happiness is also essential. Put yourself in situations where you're influenced favourably by people you know well. Seek out positive connections with others who can help you feel understood, encouraged, and part of a community.

Self-compassion is a vital skill to cultivate for times of adversity. Remember to be kind and patient with yourself as you work through the steps of lovingly detaching from a situation. Acknowledge even the smallest steps forward and be kind to yourself if you slip up or feel guilty. Keep in mind that you are worthy of contentment and joy.

Building a support system and making the difficult decision to separate from alcoholic parents is an incredibly brave and life-altering experience. Life has its ups and downs, but if you put your own needs first, establish healthy boundaries, reach out to others for help, and cultivate self-compassion, you can make it better. Keep in mind that you have the ability to end your addiction and make a better life for yourself.

Examine the effects that having parents who drank had on your development

The emotional scars one receives from a childhood spent with alcoholic parents can last a lifetime. The effects permeate every facet of their lives, not just the times when they are drunk or disorderly. These scars are the result of a complex emotional and experiential web that has woven together a tapestry of grief, terror, and bafflement.

These psychological wounds stem from an all-consuming feeling of betrayal. It's common for the offspring of alcoholics to feel abandoned by the same individuals who are entrusted with their care and well-being. A deep sense of abandonment is left in the wake of a series of broken promises, unstable behaviour, and neglect. They wish for predictability yet are caught in a tempest of constant change.

Their lives are permeated by constant worry. They worry about their parents' drinking resuming, about disputes getting out of hand, and about the future. They develop a state of heightened vigilance, in which they watch their surroundings intently for any hint of impending danger. This persistent worry leaves a permanent impression, making it tough to unwind and feel secure in their connections with others.

An overpowering sense of duty is another effect of growing up with alcoholic parents. Children often have to take on adult responsibilities such as caregiving, maintaining peace, and even parenting. They learn to repress their own wants and needs in order to maintain order in their immediate environment. They are robbed of their youth because they are expected to act like adults too soon and take on responsibilities that aren't theirs.

Children of alcoholics often struggle with low self-esteem because of their upbringing. They begin to blame themselves for the disorder at home and the behaviour of their parents who are addicted to drugs. They feel responsible for the upheaval and think their parents would change if only they were superior, unique, or lovable. These emotions permeate their entire being, making them feel like they don't deserve love or happiness.

Relationships in adulthood may also reflect the influences of their upbringing. Codependent tendencies of seeking approval and validation from others at the expense of one's own well-being are a common response to the wounds inflicted by alcoholic parents. It's possible that they have trouble saying "no," are afraid of confrontation, and are reliving the same dysfunctional patterns in their relationships that plagued them as children. As they struggle with their fears of desertion and betrayal, trust becomes difficult to achieve.

Growing up with alcoholic parents leaves deep emotional wounds that take a long time to heal. In order to do so, one must face and sort through years' worth of tangled feelings, engage in therapeutic and social support, and work to restore one's sense of self-worth and resiliency. It requires relearning healthy behaviours including setting boundaries, trusting others, and having hope for a better future.

Those who have survived a childhood with alcoholic parents are remarkably resilient and strong people. Their wounds are evidence of their strength and resilience as well as memories of all they've overcome. They can overcome the pain they've experienced and find their own way to a life of love, stability, and inner peace with time, healing, and support.

Children of alcoholics often find comfort in the company of people who can relate to their struggles. When people open up to those who can relate to them, it helps legitimise their feelings and gives them a sense of community. Eventually, people are able to peel back the layers of their emotional scars in safe environments like support groups and therapy.

They realise that taking care of themselves is crucial to their recovery. They develop the habit of caring for themselves first, in every sense of the word. They can recover their sense of identity and find their own interests and passions apart from the chaos of their upbringing by partaking in activities that bring them joy and tranquilly. They practise kindness towards themselves and look for ways to expand their sense of who they are beyond the labels others placed on them as children.

Forgiveness of oneself and one's parents is essential to the healing process. It's a difficult and introspective adventure through the maze of feelings associated with their history. When people learn to forgive themselves, they are able to let go of the guilt and shame that have been holding them back. Releasing the emotional burden that has prevented people from embracing their own pleasure does not imply forgetting or justifying the agony they encountered.

Yet another obstacle is getting their parents' forgiveness. Admitting the weakness of human nature at the root of their addiction and accepting that their acts were not indicative of the value of the child are necessary first steps. What they're really doing is freeing themselves from the emotional grasp of resentment and fury, which is different from approving the damaging behaviours. The act of forgiving someone is the beginning of the process of cutting the emotional ties that keep them stuck in the past.

Children of alcoholics frequently find a surprising strength within themselves as they make their way through the healing process. They are aware of the resilience they gained from overcoming a challenging upbringing. They believe in themselves and their ability to change, shining as examples for those who are still on their own paths to recovery.

Growing up with alcoholic parents leaves emotional scars, yet those scars can become a source of strength, empathy, and insight. While scars from the past may always be with them, they can be used as symbols of triumph over adversity and the building of a better future. They may free themselves from their past and build a life of their own choice by reclaiming their lives, rewriting their narratives, and creating healthy, caring connections.

Children of alcoholics frequently make it a goal of their healing process to end the destructive pattern of substance abuse and family discord that began in their childhood. They make a conscious effort to better themselves by learning to deal with adversity in constructive ways and becoming more self-aware.

In this context, learning and knowledge are not just aids but active agents. They are trying to get to the bottom of the intergenerational transmission of addiction's destructive behaviours. By gaining an understanding of addiction, children can reflect on their own lives, identify with their parents' challenges, and learn to set healthy limits for themselves.

Children of alcoholics can gain strength via activism and awareness-building in their search for recovery. They develop a strong desire to help other people who have had similar upbringings, fight for better treatment options, and lessen the social stigma associated with addiction and its effects on families. They hope to foster a sense of belonging and encourage others to reach out for assistance by sharing their experiences.

They put an emphasis on positive, growth-promoting interactions in their own life and seek out those people actively. By learning to identify and avoid harmful interactions, they are able to protect their own mental and emotional health. They look for genuine relationships and create a close-knit circle of friends and loved ones who get them.

Children of alcoholics have a non-linear path to recovery. There will be adversity, opportunities to be vulnerable, and times when the wounds feel especially fresh. But they keep going, fortified by the achievements they've made and the resiliency they've learned to nurture. They take comfort in the notion that recovery is an ongoing process in which any progress, however slight, is cause for celebration.

As they work towards recovery, they each gain insight into the ways in which their experiences have made them special. They are capable of significant interpersonal connections due to their high levels of empathy, compassion, and comprehension. They become examples of perseverance and inspiration by sharing their stories with those still in the midst of their own healing process.

Children of alcoholics have the potential to gain insight, compassion, and strength from their experiences. They have the power to reimagine their lives and forge a path forward that does not centre on their past hurts. Every action they take is a reclamation of their lives, a celebration of their resiliency, and a symbol of the hope for recovery, development, and a better tomorrow.

Problems with trust, low self-esteem, and abandonment anxiety are examples of difficulties these people often face

Having alcoholic parents can have a lasting effect on their adult children, often causing them to struggle with a number of issues that don't go away just because they're adults. Trust problems, low self-esteem, and abandonment anxiety are common obstacles among these.

Adult offspring of alcoholics often struggle with trust, which can have serious consequences for their relationships. They may have trouble trusting people and themselves as a result of learning to navigate a world full of chaos, broken promises, and emotional upheaval. Because of the unpredictability of their parents' behaviour, it can be difficult for children to trust others. They may find it difficult to build sexual relationships, close friendships, or even professional connections because of their innate distrust of others.

Adolescents and adults who grew up in homes with alcoholism often struggle with low self-esteem. As a result of neglect, emotional abuse, or inconsistency in parenting, children raised in addicted homes can develop a low opinion of themselves. They may internalise feelings of guilt, humiliation, or inadequacy if they are constantly exposed to chaotic or harmful behaviour. As a result, they may lack self-assurance, have trouble standing up for themselves, and think they are fundamentally flawed and unworthy of happiness and love.

Adult offspring of alcoholics have a number of difficulties, one of the most prominent being a fear of abandonment. Children whose parents exhibit unpredictable behaviour may develop an irrational fear of rejection or abandonment. They may acquire an unhealthy preoccupation with being liked and accepted by others, looking for reassurance all the time and living in perpetual terror that their loved ones would abandon them. Clinginess, possessiveness, and an unwillingness to set healthy boundaries are all ways that people with a fear of abandonment can negatively impact their relationships, making it hard for them to form lasting, trusted bonds with others.

These problems compound and feed off of one another, making life difficult for the adult offspring of alcoholics. If they have trouble trusting others, it can be difficult for them to build healthy relationships, which can further lower their self-esteem and heighten their fear of abandonment. Getting to the bottom of these problems and recovering from the hurts of their upbringing takes introspection, therapy, and a community of compassionate people who can listen, validate, and aid in the restoration of trust. It is possible for adult children of alcoholic parents to overcome these obstacles and build healthier, more rewarding lives for themselves with time, patience, and the right assistance.

Adult offspring of alcoholics frequently struggle with a variety of issues stemming from their childhood, including trust problems, low self-esteem, and a fear of abandonment.

Responsibility and the need to exert control over one's surroundings are two such difficulties. Hyper-vigilance is a common coping mechanism among those who have grown up in unstable situations. They may take on the position of carer or mediator in the household, placing an undue emphasis on their own well-being in order to ensure the happiness of others around them. They may have trouble delegating work and avoid circumstances where they feel they have little influence as adults because of their ingrained demand for control. For them, trusting others and relinquishing control can be a huge challenge.

The inability to open up about feelings is another obstacle. Adult offspring of alcoholics may have experienced or watched their parent's emotional volatility, making them hesitant of showing their own sensitivity. Because of past experiences with hurt or rejection, they may have learnt to repress their feelings or construct emotional walls. This can make it hard for them to form close relationships or ask for help when they need it because they aren't sure how to describe how they feel. A person's development can be greatly aided by learning techniques for expressing and accepting their emotions.

Having trouble drawing the line is a persistent problem for many adult children of alcoholic parents. If they were raised in a home where boundaries were routinely crossed or ignored, it's possible that they'll never learn how to set and stick to healthy ones in their adult relationships. They may have trouble setting boundaries, struggle to say "no," or have trouble differentiating between their own wants and requirements. They must learn to be more forceful and to set healthy limits for their own good and the sake of their relationships.

To overcome these obstacles, one must look inward, seek out expert advice, and surround oneself with others who care. Validation, understanding, and healing tools can be gained through therapy, support groups, and networking with others who have gone through similar circumstances. Adult offspring of alcoholics can find resilience, inner strength, and the freedom to live the life they envision if they are honest about the effects of their childhood and commit to their own development.

Adult offspring of alcoholics sometimes struggle with intimacy and developing close, trusting relationships. They may have trouble with both emotional and physical closeness as a result of growing up in an environment marked by instability and failed relationships. They might have learned to isolate themselves to avoid more hurt or rejection. This can make them wary of letting their guard down around other people, which in turn makes it harder for them to develop genuine connections with others.

Many adult children of alcoholics also struggle with self-care and neglect issues. If they were raised in a home where they weren't prioritised, they may view their own happiness as less significant than the happiness of those around them. This might show up as a tendency towards self-neglect, difficulties prioritising one's own needs, and excessive focus on the needs of others. It is critical for their long-term health and happiness that they learn to put themselves first and to set appropriate limits on their own care.

Adult children of alcoholics may also struggle with financial insecurity. Addiction's monetary costs can have far-reaching implications on a family's standard of life, increasing the risk of bankruptcy, default, or homelessness. This might lead to worry and unease about one's financial situation. Getting out of this rut and into more sustainable financial practises may benefit from education, coaching, and expert assistance.

Chapter seven

Therapy

Healing treatments for adult children of alcoholic parents involve a wide range of methods for fostering mental health and coping with the specific difficulties these people have faced throughout their lives. These methods offer a safe space for people to reflect on and overcome the effects of their upbringing, making them stronger and more capable as a result.

Therapy is a vital part of the recovery process. Adult offspring of alcoholics benefit from individual treatment because it provides a confidential setting in which they can explore their own thoughts, feelings, and behaviours. Understanding how their upbringing has shaped who they are now allows them to create more healthy coping techniques. People can process trauma, work through emotional blocks, and further their personal development using approaches including CBT, psychodynamic therapy, and family systems therapy.

The benefits of group therapy or support groups for adult children of alcoholic parents are often magnified when they are designed with their unique needs in mind. In these kinds of environments, you can find comfort and understanding from people who can relate to what you're going through. Individuals benefit from hearing others' experiences because it helps them feel heard and validated. In addition to receiving emotional and practical assistance, support groups are a great place to make relationships with like-minded people and gain new perspectives.

Taking care of oneself is an essential part of getting better. Taking the time to care for oneself on a daily basis is beneficial for one's mental, emotional, and spiritual health. This may require doing things like setting firm limits, learning to meditate or practise mindfulness, working out regularly, eating well, and getting plenty of shut-eye. Keeping a journal can be an effective method of introspection and dealing with difficult feelings. Hobbies and other forms of creative expression provide people with a means of self-expression and a means of finding happiness independent of their immediate environment. One must also take care of oneself by engaging in healthy interpersonal interactions and actively seeking out social support.

Adult offspring of alcoholics can benefit from counselling, support groups, and self-care practises, but they can also use educational resources to learn more about addiction, codependency, and the effects of their childhood. One can gain understanding and learn to view oneself and one's parents with more compassion by reading books on the topic, going to workshops or listening to podcasts on the issue.

The road to recovery for the adult offspring of alcoholics is different for everyone. A journey of discovery, growth, and healing can be started with the help of therapy, support groups, self-care practises, and educational resources. They can overcome their past, build a better present, and take charge of their future with time, resilience, and a strong support system.

In the course of their recovery, patients may find it helpful to experiment with various therapy approaches until they find the one(s) that best meet their unique requirements and preferences. Some people may benefit from non-verbal methods of communication such as art therapy, music therapy, or dance therapy. These artistic practises can be a wonderful way to find peace and new perspectives within yourself.

Healing can also be aided by mind-body techniques like yoga and tai chi. These methods incorporate physical movement, breathwork, and mindfulness to help you unwind, lessen your stress, and become more in tune with yourself. Individuals can gain a sense of grounding and power by reestablishing a connection between their minds and bodies through practises like yoga and meditation.

Healing can be aided by investigating one's spirituality or engaging in practises that are consistent with one's beliefs. A sense of meaning, purpose, and connection to something higher than oneself can be found through spirituality, whether through prayer, meditation, attending religious services, or interacting with nature.

Equine-assisted therapy and wilderness therapy are two examples of experiential therapies that may be useful in certain situations. The therapy process in these approaches includes interaction with animals or the natural environment. Spending time in nature, or with horses, may be a powerful catalyst for personal development, trust-building, and introspection.

It's crucial to remember that recovery is a process, not a destination, and that different methods will speak to different people at various points along the way. Some people prefer to use a variety of methods at once, while others prefer to specialise. Self-care, self-compassion, and dedication to one's own development are the keys to success.

In the end, the therapeutic approaches used to treat adult offspring of alcoholic parents are as unique as the people who need help. Individuals can progressively recover from their past hurts and forge a present and future marked by resilience, self-discovery, and empowerment by adopting a holistic approach that addresses emotional, physical, and spiritual well-being.

Individuals may choose to pursue additional paths of development and metamorphosis as they continue on their recovery journey. This can entail going on a retreat or attending a session for those who come from alcoholic families. These all-encompassing adventures provide excellent chances for contemplation, education from authorities, and human connection. They have the potential to serve as a focal point for introspection and recovery.

Creating positive coping mechanisms and strengthening resilience are also crucial to the recovery process. This could entail practising relaxation methods like deep breathing, meditation, or progressive muscle relaxation to handle stressful situations. Building resilience through the practise of positive coping skills equips people to face the inevitable difficulties of life with more health and equilibrium.

Codependency issues, if any, may also need to be addressed and resolved during the healing process. Adopting caregiving roles or engaging in destructive practises of enabling or seeking acceptance are common pathways to codependency within an alcoholic family structure. Codependency counselling or support groups can help individuals recognise their destructive behaviours and learn new ways of relating to themselves and others.

The act of forgiving oneself or someone also plays a vital role in recovery. What forgiveness is about is releasing oneself from the emotional burden of resentment and hatred, not condoning or forgetting the past. Forgiveness can be explored in therapy or via introspection as a way for people to heal from past hurts and move on with their lives.

Some people who have recovered from traumatic events decide to help others who are going through the same thing. Participating in advocacy work, helping with support groups, or simply sharing one's own story can all serve to uplift and encourage others. By showing compassion and understanding, members of the community can help end the destructive cycle of alcoholism and foster recovery.

Keep in mind that everyone is different and that there is no cookie-cutter solution to mending. Each person must move at their own pace and meet their own requirements, asking for help when they feel stuck. By taking a holistic approach to recovery, people can keep developing and thriving while also shaping their own futures in ways that aren't limited by their experiences.

Chapter eight

Romantic relationships

The effects of having grown up in an alcoholic home on a person's romantic life can be devastating. It can be difficult to counteract the impacts of such an atmosphere on one's outlook, expectations, and actions.

The lack of confidence between parties is the primary problem. Trust is easily damaged in an alcoholic home because of the alcoholic's tendency to break promises, act erratically, and keep everyone guessing about what he or she will do next. This can make it difficult for people raised in such environments to totally trust their romantic partners. They may have trouble trusting their partner because they are afraid of being abandoned or abandoned again, just as they were as children.

People who have an alcoholic parent or guardian typically feel the burden of adult responsibilities at an early age. It's possible that they had to grow up quickly in order to care for an alcoholic parent or sibling, run the household, or handle emotional or mental distress. They may experience an excessive urge to take care of their companions, manage the situation, or avoid confrontations at all costs, and this sense of duty might follow them into their love relationships. This can cause them to develop unhealthy patterns of codependence in which their own needs and those of their significant others are routinely overlooked.

Dysfunctional styles of interaction are common among people who grew up in alcoholic homes. It's possible that there was a lack of open and honest communication, and that disagreements were typically resolved through avoidance, manipulation, or explosive outbursts. As a result, people from these backgrounds may have difficulty communicating their feelings, standing up for what they need, and settling problems amicably. They may experience anxiety or dread of confrontation, which causes them to repress their emotions or avoid having difficult conversations.

An individual's sense of pride and value in themselves is another factor that may be altered. Neglect, emotional abuse, and inconsistent parenting are common experiences for children of alcoholic parents or guardians. Feelings of inadequacy, shame, or worthlessness can result from such situations, leaving behind severe emotional scars. People who grew up in such settings may have an unhealthy need for the love and acceptance of their romantic partners. They may fear being alone or think they don't deserve better, making them more likely to stick to relationships despite their unpleasant or toxic nature.

Understanding the effects of growing up in an alcoholic home and taking steps to improve romantic relationships is essential for development. Individuals can recover from trauma, learn effective coping skills, set healthy boundaries, and increase trust and closeness in their relationships through therapy, support groups, and introspective thinking. A dedication to self-awareness, healing, and personal growth is necessary to break the cycle and create rewarding, loving interactions.

One's capacity for self-control may be further hampered if they grew up in an alcoholic home. Emotions, from anger and annoyance to sadness and perplexity, tend to run high in alcoholic households. Young children who are exposed to such displays may have difficulty regulating their own emotions. Because of their inability to openly communicate their emotions, they may have trouble developing close bonds with their romantic relationships.

People who grew up in alcoholic homes may have trouble with both emotional regulation and attachment and intimacy issues. An insecure attachment style could have resulted from their carers' lack of predictability or consistency. As a result, they may have trouble trusting their partners and developing strong emotional attachments with them. Problems arise when one spouse has an unhealthy fear of desertion or an unhealthy obsession with being physically close to their mate.

Growing up in an alcoholic home can have far-reaching consequences, including problems with substance abuse and addiction. Those who have seen the devastating effects of alcoholism on others may be more prone to substance misuse or destructive behaviour as a means of coping with their own emotional suffering. Addiction is prioritised over the demands of their partners and the relationship, which can put a strain on their romantic connections.

Growing up in an alcoholic home has a wide-ranging and nuanced effect on romantic partnerships. It affects a person's trust, communication styles, sense of self-worth, and capacity to develop secure ties, among other things. Even while these things can be difficult, it's crucial to keep in mind that they don't determine your fate. Individuals can overcome these obstacles and create loving relationships based on trust, mutual respect, and emotional closeness with the help of self-awareness, support, and a dedication to personal progress.

An alcoholic's romantic choices may mirror the disorder and instability that characterise the disease. People who grew up in tumultuous environments may be attracted to others who have similar addictive tendencies or chaotic behaviours. They may subconsciously look for companions who remind them of happier times, even though doing so would be a recurrence of dysfunctional habits. To break the cycle, you must first become self-aware and then be prepared to question and alter long-held ways of relating to others.

People who grew up in alcoholic homes are more likely to have problems with good boundary-setting in romantic relationships. Young people who have encountered inconsistent care and hazy boundaries may find it difficult to set firm limits and advocate for their own needs as adults. They may put their own needs and ideals on the back burner in order to meet their partner's expectations or avoid arguments. Establishing appropriate boundaries and making time for one's own self-care become essential skills for maintaining harmony in interpersonal interactions.

Keep in mind that not everyone who grew up in an alcoholic home will face these difficulties in the same ways or to the same degrees. Resilience, social networks, and intentional self-improvement are just a few of the aspects that contribute to an individual's distinct reaction. Individuals can heal from the negative effects of their upbringing via introspection, therapy, and a dedication to change. This allows them to form healthy connection patterns that promote love, trust, and emotional well-being.

Chapter nine

Difficulties that adult offspring of alcoholic parents encounter while starting their own families

Becoming a parent is a rewarding and life-altering experience for anyone, but for adult children of alcoholic parents, it can present special problems. One's emotional health and capacity to handle the stresses of parenthood might take a serious hit if they were raised in an alcoholic household.

To begin, adult offspring of alcoholic parents frequently have difficulty overcoming emotional issues that were first experienced as youngsters. They may have suffered from emotional scarring due to neglect, inconsistency, or even abuse. When they have children of their own, they may experience a reawakening of these unhealed wounds as they struggle with anxieties of repeating the same patterns or failing to create a supportive environment.

In addition, adult offspring of alcoholics may be burdened by feelings of mistrust and insecurity. They may have experienced or observed unstable behaviour, unfulfilled promises, or damaged relationships, and as a result, they have learned to distrust others and even themselves. This can make it hard for them to form emotionally safe bonds with their own children and keep relationships strong. They may distrust their own parenting skills and suffer with emotions of inadequacy.

Moreover, defence strategies like hypervigilance or emotional suppression learned as children might become roadblocks when confronted with the duties of motherhood. It can be challenging for adult children of alcoholic parents to find a middle ground between keeping their children safe and encouraging them to develop their own identities. Because they have learnt to put their own needs last in order to focus on the needs of others, they may also have difficulty expressing their feelings or reaching out for help when they need it.

Problems may also arise due to a dearth of positive examples to emulate. It's possible that they didn't have any good examples of parenting or healthy role models while growing up in an alcoholic home. They may feel unprepared for the challenges of parenting and have difficulty setting limits, enforcing discipline consistently, and creating a safe and secure home for their children.

Adult children of alcoholic parents frequently confront the challenge of keeping in touch with a parent who is battling alcoholism. Emotional upheaval can arise when a person struggles to protect their children from harm while also feeling sympathy and loyalty towards their parent.

Despite these difficulties, adult children of alcoholics should go for help and healing. They can find a secure place to work through their feelings, gain perspective on their upbringing, and pick up useful techniques for parenting through therapy, support groups, or counselling. Having a group of friends, a partner, or other family members to lean on may be a great source of comfort and advice for new parents.

Adult offspring of alcoholics have the ability to break the cycle and provide a caring and stable environment for their own children, despite the special challenges they may confront. They may overcome these obstacles and provide a pleasant and loving environment for both themselves and their children if they focus on self-awareness, self-care, and healing.

Adult children of alcoholics may take comfort in the chance to rewrite their family story as they begin their own parenting adventure. They can provide a better, more stable home life for their kids without the stigma of drug abuse and homelessness. Because of this insight, they may choose to parent with greater purpose and deliberation.

Adult offspring of alcoholics can bring a great deal of empathy to their own parenting. They may be more attuned to their children's feelings and wants because they have been through similar experiences. An atmosphere of mutual understanding and compassion can be established when a parent is able to put themselves in their child's shoes.

The upbringing they had from their alcoholic parents may have given them the tools they need to overcome adversity and adjust to new situations. Because of the challenges they've overcome, they may be better able to solve problems and adjust to new conditions than others. These traits can be especially helpful as they navigate the ups and downs of parenthood.

Understanding the significance of self-care for adult children of alcoholic parents is also essential. They may have seen what happens when people stop taking care of themselves and can use this knowledge to set healthy examples for their own children. They can show their kids the value of self-care by doing things for themselves that boost their own mental and emotional well-being.

Adult children of alcoholics can also seek out books, websites, and workshops to help them become better parents themselves. Helpful advice on positive methods of discipline, open lines of communication, and fostering a safe space can be found in these materials. By actively seeking knowledge and resources, they can close the gap between their own upbringing and the ideal style of parenting they hope to instill in their children.

It's important to make friends and allies along the way. Support groups for adult children of alcoholics provide a safe space to talk to others who understand their situation. The ability to confide in, seek guidance from, and feel validated by those who have experienced similar struggles is a powerful source of strength and solace.

For adult offspring of alcoholic parents, becoming parents is a life-altering journey. They'll need to do some introspective soul-searching, mend some broken hearts, and hone their parenting skills. They may break the cycle of addiction and dysfunction and create a better, more loving future for themselves and their children through introspection, self-compassion, and a dedication to growth.

On their way to becoming parents themselves, adult offspring of alcoholics may continue to experience recurrent triggers and vulnerable times. The parents' personal experiences and feelings may resurface in response to particular events or developmental milestones in their children's lives. They should recognise these triggers and treat themselves gently as they go through them.

Being a parent can also help them mend emotionally. The pressure to provide a safe and stable environment for their children may prompt them to address emotional wounds from their own childhood. They might decide to see a therapist or counsellor to go through any unresolved trauma or harmful worldviews that could affect how they parent. By engaging in self-reflection and healing, individuals can end the transmission of trauma from one generation to the next and leave a better world for the next generation.

Adult offspring of alcoholics may also find it difficult to set limits with their own alcoholic parents. They may feel compelled to limit their alcoholic parents' access to their children in order to shield them from damage. To protect their own family unit, it may be necessary to create space between them or even cut off contact, which can be an emotionally taxing and challenging process. While navigating these intricate connections, it is crucial that they put their children's physical and mental well-being first.

Adult offspring of alcoholics may also face prejudice and misinformation about the disease of addiction and its effects on families. People who don't have any compassion or understanding for them may judge or scrutinise them. This can be emotionally draining and a source of isolation. They can find affirmation, encouragement, and a sense of belonging by surrounding themselves with supportive friends, family, or support groups.

Adult children of alcoholics may have learned the value of honest and open communication with their own families as a result of their own upbringing. They might make it a point to foster an atmosphere where their kids are at ease voicing their thoughts and feelings. They recognise the importance of giving their kids a place where they can open up without worrying about what others would think.

Adult offspring of alcoholic parents confront particular problems, but they also have a chance to stop the cycle of addiction and provide a safe, loving home for their own children. They can become strong, caring parents who provide their kids the love, stability, and direction they need by facing their demons, getting help from others, and building resilience.

For adult offspring of alcoholic parents, being a parent is a life-altering experience that calls for constant introspection, care for one's own needs, and a determination to alter destructive habits. It's a brave move that might leave a lasting legacy of love and support for future generations, improving the quality of life for everyone involved.

Give them advice on how to stop doing things the wrong way and start caring for their own kids.

Individuals who were raised by alcoholic parents may find it difficult but necessary to break unfavourable parenting practises and provide a supportive atmosphere for their own children. Their own approach to parenting may be profoundly influenced by their own childhood experiences of neglect, inconsistency, or abuse. It is possible, however, for parents to break out of these ruts via deliberate action and introspection and provide a loving home for their kids.

Awareness of one's own poor parenting tendencies is the first step towards changing those tendencies. Those who were brought up by alcoholics must take stock of their lives and identify any negative habits they may have picked up from their parents. In doing so, they will examine how their experiences have affected them emotionally and intellectually. They can start destroying their bad habits and replacing them with good ones after they have a firm grasp on where those habits originated.

Finding a community of people who believe in you is crucial while trying to quit bad habits. Therapy, support groups, and confiding in close friends and family are just a few examples. Therapists are trained professionals who may aid patients in working through difficult emotions, learning new coping skills, and even learning how to be a better parent. A sense of belonging and validation can be found in the company of others who have been through something similar, and this is what support groups are all about.

Another important stage is getting education on how to be a good parent. Positive parenting approaches can be learned by reading books, articles, attending workshops, or consulting online resources. They can learn more about how to establish healthy boundaries, communicate effectively, and form secure ties with their kids. They can learn new techniques to make their home a safe and happy place for their children.

Self-care is essential for changing dysfunctional parenting habits. When parents prioritise their own emotional, mental, and physical health, they are better able to meet their children's needs. Individuals can better control their emotions, reduce stress, and foster a more stable and loving family environment by partaking in activities that offer them joy and fulfilment, practising mindfulness or meditation, and placing a high priority on self-reflection.

One of the most important aspects of changing dysfunctional parenting habits is opening out to one's kids. The trust between parents and their children grows and deepens when the home is a place where kids may talk freely about how they're feeling without worrying about being reprimanded. By showing their children empathy and actively listening to what they have to say, parents may help their children develop emotionally and foster open lines of communication within the family.

It is also important to establish firm limits and operate under a uniform set of guidelines. When adults set and maintain high standards for their children, the kids benefit greatly. Parents may help their kids feel secure and safe by setting acceptable limits on their behaviour. Consequences and rewards for staying within these bounds should be fair, considerate, and oriented towards educating and guiding rather than punishing.

Establishing a loving home and eliminating destructive parenting habits requires setting a good example for children. Those who grew up with alcoholic parents have the power to model those traits for their own children. By emulating these qualities themselves, parents set a good example for their kids and impart invaluable wisdom.

A caring atmosphere can be fostered in part by establishing routines and maintaining stability within the family. Predictability in the form of set mealtimes, nighttime routines, and quality family time helps children feel safe and secure. Children benefit greatly from parents who are consistent in their discipline techniques, expectations, and punishments.

Parents' sensitivity to their kids' feelings and needs is essential. Parents may assist their kids become emotionally intelligent and confident by acknowledging and validating their feelings. Parents can deepen their relationships with their children by taking the time to listen to, and empathise with, their children's feelings.

Those who were brought up by alcoholics should be aware of their own emotional triggers and reactions as parents. Understanding when parents are projecting their own unresolved pain onto their children is crucial. Parents can break the cycle of passing on their unresolved concerns to their children by learning self-regulation strategies and getting counselling or assistance.

Building a community of caring adults, whether they are friends, relatives, or other parents, can be an invaluable resource. Negative parenting habits are difficult to break, but they may be managed with the help of stories, guidance, and lessons from others who have been there.

Parents who themselves grew up with alcoholism should be kind and patient with themselves as they make this difficult transition. Negative parenting habits are not easy to break, and there will likely be setbacks along the way. Never lose sight of the fact that any and all progress, no matter how slight, deserves to be recognised and praised.

Parents should keep in mind that their efforts to create a warm home for their children are only one part of who they are. They can choose to do something different for their offspring and interrupt the cycle of negativity. They may reimagine themselves as parents and create a brighter future for their children if they focus on their strengths, resilience, and ability to adapt.

It's possible that parents will learn the value of self-forgiveness as they work to alter destructive ways of parenting. They should be kind to themselves and realise that they are doing the best they can with the knowledge and skills they have. Parents can better nurture an environment of love, support, and understanding by letting go of guilt or self-blame and focusing instead on development and learning.

Parents who themselves grew up with alcoholism should, above all else, treat their children with love and compassion and work hard to end the cycle of alcoholism and dysfunction in their own families. By actively deciding to provide their children the love, security, and support they may have lacked as children, parents may cultivate a setting that fosters their children's emotional health, resilience, and social development.

Negative parenting habits can only be broken and a nurturing environment can only be created through consistent introspection, education, and development. Parents may emerge from the shadows of their past and build a future of love, healing, and great family dynamics with devotion, perseverance, and a genuine desire to provide the best possible upbringing for their children.

Printed in Great Britain
by Amazon

29810172R00066